DELICACIES

THOSE THAT MADE MY LIFE "MINE"

PUJA S. ROY

ISBN 979-888530769-7

To my parents,

Who have always stood by my side

Contents

Contents

Foreword

Life is not merely the act of surviving. It is the act of living.

Often at times, we're told stories of births and of deaths. But what makes our lives "ours" are the "in-betweens". They're the ones which shape us and give us a purpose in our life. However, what is it that happens after we die? Do we remember our past life? Do we relate to it even then? Or do we end up forgetting the people who had left an impression in our lives?

It's finally about time I discovered the real delicacies of my life.

Acknowledgements

I thank everyone who has left an impression in my life- in some way or the other.

From my friends at school to the ones I now have lost my touch with, I'm ever grateful to the almighty for providing me the luxury of being born in this world.

The remaining few days

Not being certain as to when I'd see you again,

If not in this life, perhaps in the next.

It is some misery to have nothing to cling to,

Despite you being here,

It seems as if I'm devouring my own solitude.

Drowning in my hypothetical tributaries,

I keep ricocheting between my miseries.

For what would I be left to feed upon,

Living a life devoid of you, regardless of your presence.

You being here near me isn't enough anymore to keep me sane.

Things can't go on their own for I'll be left to dissipate,

I needed you to pull me away from this asininity.

And you've failed me...

If only you could've made me veer off my course,

You'd have been the "messiah" I'd been looking for all this time.

No longer do I need you, no longer are you eligible for that appellation.

It's all over now,

The remaining few days, I'm obliged to live life as an insouciant loner.

- *Doesn't relate to the title? Keep reading to see what does!*

Late by a minute

I tried my best and gave my best

I travelled roads towards the west.

Made myself accustomed to the zest

More than the pain within my chest.

I laughed with some cowards

Cried among the city's boulevards

Where in the depths I pushed it inward.

A minute gone by seconds outward.

I learned to rush, to gain my speed

I finished my work without paying heed

All of which just to take the lead

To turn my back at my own need.

Sometime around May

I was being choked to death

By the one who held the rope for me

It had been long enough

Perhaps he was just exhausted

Exhausted enough to let go of certainty

Hence, he loosened his grip on the rope

And I…

Fell

Into the abyss, into the incessant loop

Dubiousness, hesitancy: here we come.

It was hard to breathe at first

Without my man— it felt uncanny

But then I realized, there's an afterlife, too.

I rushed towards the door of numbness

To numb my affinity, infatuation, etc, etc.

So, I did, and at last, gained equilibrium.

I sat to cry, by the banks of Nile

I left my hometown earlier that day,

Sick of hearing the words that they say.

"To where?", a curious friend of mine had asked.

I was so tired that I ignored it and basked.

People, all they do, is always bring me down.

Not leaving back then would've had me drown.

Their bitter words ricocheted between my head

All day long and living was the same as being dead.

I arrived at my destination where nobody knew me,

Did what I wanted to while sitting under a tree.

I sat having the longest river by my side,

So, it could conveniently lend my tears a place to hide.

Remembering all the trash they once said,

I cried my heart out, and emptied the trash in my head.

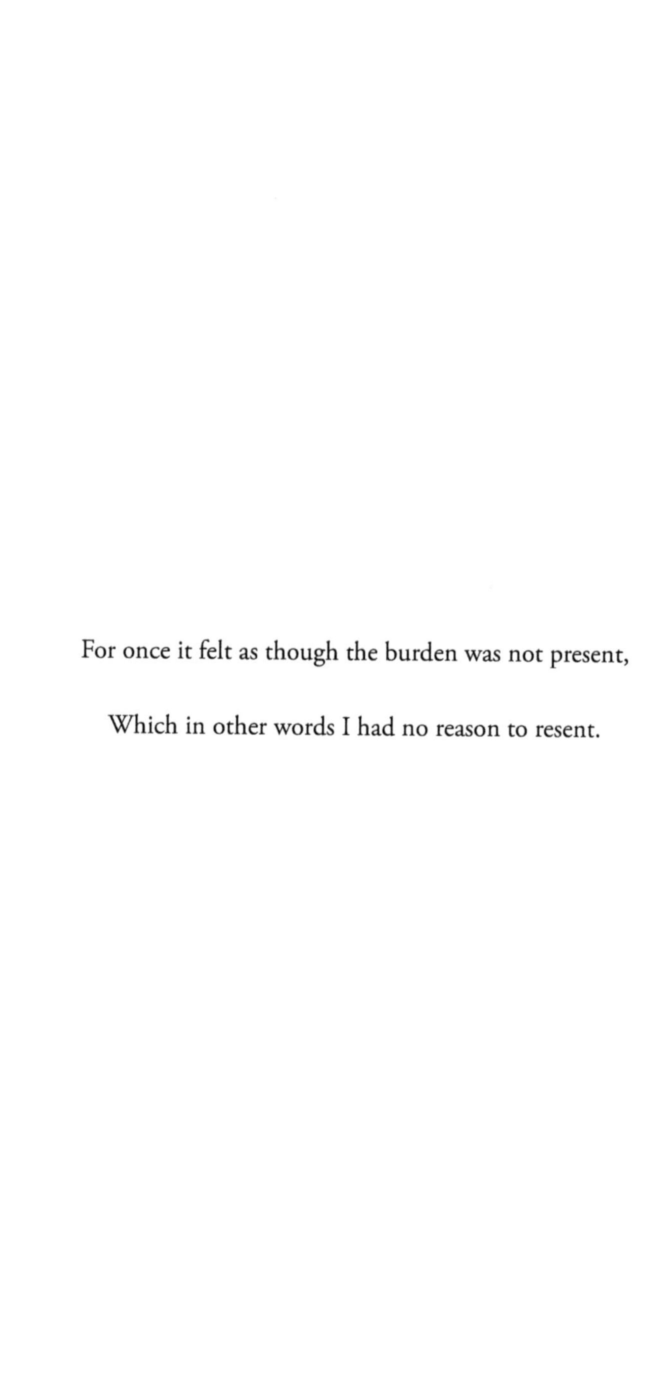

For once it felt as though the burden was not present,

Which in other words I had no reason to resent.

The day the sun within me died

Tired of shining,

Tired of sharing the light,

Tired of spreading hope,

There came a day

When the nearest star

Stopped shining.

It stopped spreading light.

It stopped making efforts

To make others happy.

But that was the day

When it started shining

For its own self...

The light wasn't visible

To anyone else

But the sun was happy

"Better off dead" worked.

Reincarnation

Who are we after all?

Level one of life: to be born

From being inside the mother's womb

To making it alive out of the dark inside,

We are born as innate winners.

Then we learn to laugh, smile and talk

Soon we know how to sit and walk

It's just we take birth and keep progressing.

Just to die in the end hearing unwanted cries.

But in the short span of life when we're tied up

We hurt people through our avoidable lies.

Within the very few limited years of life

We end up slaughtering so many other lives

Perhaps thinking being born as a human

Is the ultimate achievement one can do

And to make full use of it in this life

Is the best thing one must be doing.

Selfishness, ruthlessness, acquisitiveness

All of which heavily contribute

To the barbaric slaughterhouse of mankind

As if all of this makes us what we are, homo sapiens

And if success doesn't knock on a lenient man's doors.

We butcher one animal and despite committing a sin

Blame one for butchering the others

As if one life overweighs the other

Despite knowing how futile it is

To make enemies instead of brothers.

Growing up in a judgemental society

Where life holds varied values

We have all been willingly or unwillingly settling

For something too trifling and meaningless

Each of us was born naive and innocent

But in the course of time we grow up to be cold

With the passage of time,

We lost the kindness that makes us earthlings

Just to be able to fit perfectly in a society

That teaches us who can be bought and sold .

Life has different definitions

So, it all depends on who you ask

'Cause some spend their lives

Trying hard enough to impress others

But some make themselves their topmost priority

And live all of their life to the fullest.

Who are we to judge a living being?

Being alive today and dead tomorrow,

Why not stop having selfish attributes

Since in the end we're nothing more than

A reason of someone's sorrow

And an occupant of the underground.

In another life

I would tell my mother

That I loved her unconditionally.

I would pay off my dad's debts

And let him know that I'm there.

I would let that special someone know

He was the one I loved the most.

I would extend my thanks to teachers

For whom I achieved what I did.

I would do the things

I was too scared to take up.

I would live each day

As if I were to die the next.

I would do some deeds

Worth all the nostalgia.

I would set world records

To acquaint people with my name.

But until I'm reborn,

These shall remain as words

Between you and me

Shh, keep quiet.

Advices from my current life

Don't gawk at anything for too long

Every being gets bored of everything.

Don't think of your castle as an exception

Staring at it for too long makes it a victim of deception.

Don't waste hours ameliorating its beauty

For it never pretermitted its duty.

Don't try to let loose the shackles

Instead, do realize they were the cause of your cackles.

Don't let greed feed upon you to destroy you

We all know how it has never dragged a man to his destiny

Don't permit yourself to mess with dear fate

Deep down you already know your castle is your true mate.

Shattered memories from my past life-

Beyond the fever of love

In a world where love isn't about two people being blindfolded,

Where it isn't about running away from reality but considering it well enough.

Where logic plays its part perfectly and life continues to make sense,

And sanity, it remains, despite walking those extra miles for each other.

And no matter how contagious melancholy may seem,

There are people who shall never forget the significance of harmony,

And despite breathing in the same atmosphere of their own misery and mood swings,

They are known to be sharing the weight and holding hands, though hanging from different strings.

Had it been an existing world, I would've loved you infinitely, beyond my capabilities.

But as of now, I keep my desires away from you, in secretion.

Just to fit well in this society where love is known to drive people crazy and leave them in the dark.

And where we are taught that life is the same with or without a person willing to walk with us.

Stars of this new world

Blinking memories from worlds apart

Horrors and miseries all mixed with love

Days pass by with no sign of reappearance

The remaining ones, divided by abhorrence.

Stars aren't known to portray feelings

But neither are they mere drops of lights

They might very well be embodiments

Of blissful love, withering loss and connections

What a lovely sight, it turns out to be!

With so many people looking above

And associating those twinkling bodies

With a long-lost person, they once knew of.

The queen from my past life

FLAWED YET BEAUTIFUL

She's flawed

Wears her scars with pride

Fills her mind with applaud

& dreams of reaching heights.

She fought well

Bravely enough

For she keeps those scars

As a reminder of her last fight.

The latest one

Energizes each cell of her body

& fills her up

With reminders of victory.

Those wounds of hers

Grant access to the light

To penetrate inside her bones

& hype her up.

To make her aware

Of who she is

The queen who fought

& the girl who triumphed.

Doors of this world

There are some doors

That we can't walk through

They're meant to be seen

But not to be crossed.

Doors that remain mysterious

Until the end of time

And ask us to leave them

Alone, in this dark world.

These are the doors

Equivalent to show pieces

That mothers buy for us

But never let us touch.

Giving birth to questions

Thousands of them lie

Unanswered, as they are

Buried underneath to die.

Missing my past life

Would it make sense to you?

If I say I've had this longing for home

That doesn't exist. Not yet, to me.

One which I feel a connection to

Unlike all I've been in with the same regret.

I've seen too many buildings

Coated with cement on top of bricks

Lived in a few of them too,

But with nothing worth being homesick.

These have together made me nomadic

And expanded my longing with time

To build a home full of comfort

In the vast stretches of this sphere.

What I know to be the "society"

I have come across too many people expressing their dissatisfaction with our so-called society. The ones whom my opinions completely align with and I should make the least effort to express dissent for. The question here arises "why" would I? Why would I disapprove of something you approve? And when I'm cognizant of being as literate as the ones around me. However, in between all this, forgetting that everyone in our society, though with a few exceptions, considers their opinions to be the reason for their exultation. As an embodiment of pride and glory.

Had they been united enough to acknowledge the similarities in their way of thinking, our society could've been ameliorated. But modern people, these days, refuse to be considered ordinary. They refuse to be a part of this wonted society when unknowingly they're the superior ones in our society, the ones shaping and influencing this society of ours. What these people know as being cool is a part of them depriving themselves of their competence.

But perhaps this is what life is all about. That's the society we're used to being a part of. But oh, I wish one day these "cool" people can welcome an uncool change and finally accept that they're born in a society that is good enough. Which nourishes them and provides them ample resources to nourish themselves and their successors in the future. And one which grants them the

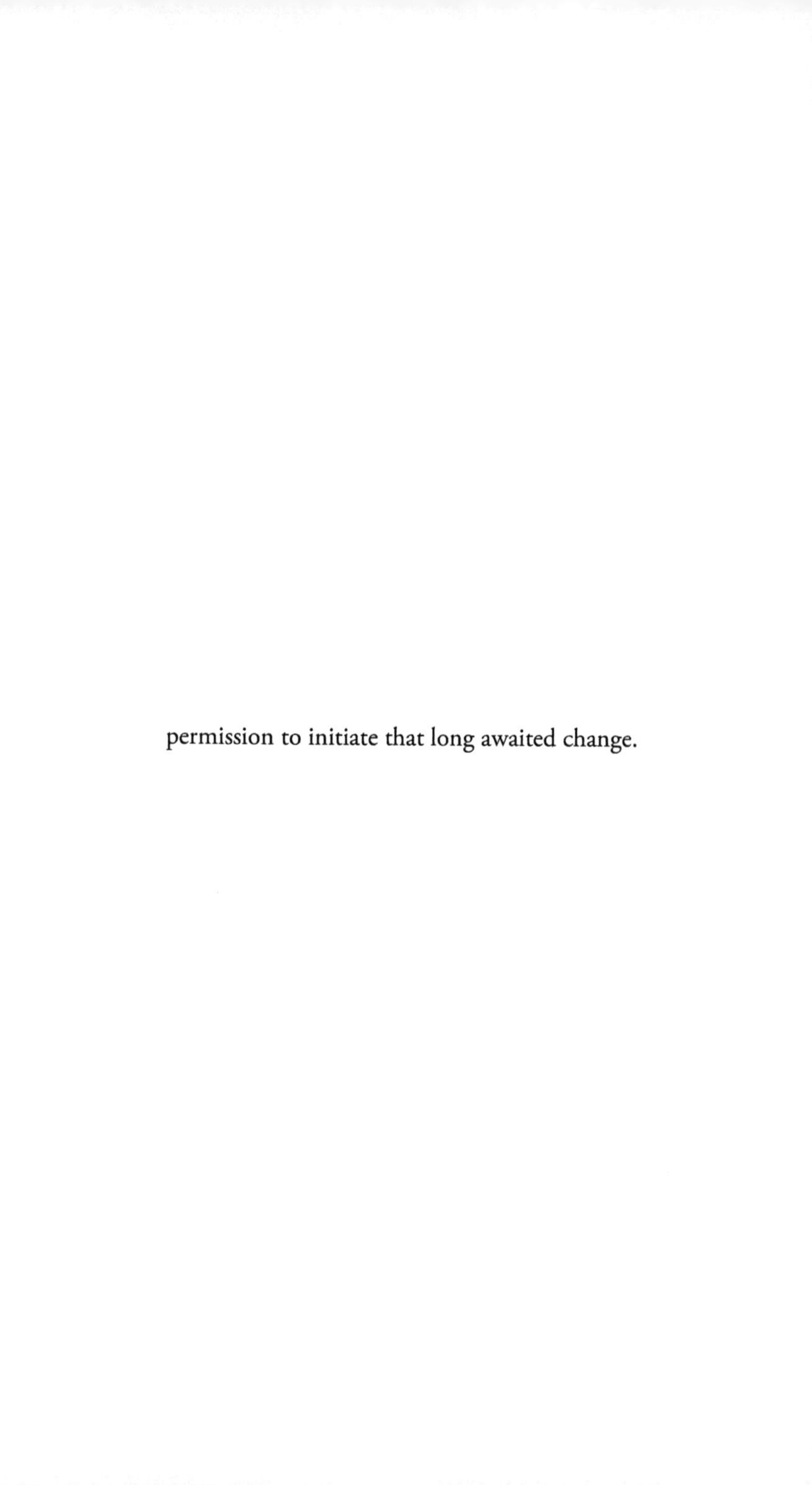

permission to initiate that long awaited change.

Losing the will to live again

I make a note of all those who care

Wondering if someone plays fair.

If in this life one makes an effort

To provide me with some comfort.

Despite knowing my own worth

I don't prefer to light the hearth.

I do know how badly people suck

And then make you believe in luck.

All-day long it provokes me to burst

In tears and I lie there at my worst.

Still expecting someone to show up

Someone who can empty the cup.

And then not keep it as a reminder

To tell me they helped me surrender.

Then at times, it all comes crashing

Cognizing me how it seems smashing.

What to do and what not to do

Are the answers I can never pursue.

Live and let others live are the words

Which cut me each time like swords

How can I let others live in peace?

When each day I want my life to cease.

I don't care if it even sounds selfish

For all I want is this body to perish.

This is life and this is how I play my game

Unlike the ones wanting just fame.

I get reminded of my predictions from my past life

"The thought of you losing interest in me someday emotionally crippples me.

Knowing that nothing lasts for eternities carves a hole in my heart each day

And do you know what hurts the most?

Being aware of the fact that our love isn't an exception to this fact.

I wish it were… I wish I could make it last forever.

And that sucks too. Me continuing to wish despite knowing how all these wishes

Will probably never come true."

Cleansed blood

Men in this world never question their own purity

But find it better to doubt the women they say they love.

Ironically, a woman, in turn, overlooks the man's flaws

Just so she could let him be the only one she worships.

- *From a time I met someone who was questioned about her "purity"*

The day that never ends

Incognizant of what tomorrow has in store for me

I go to bed and want the bedbugs to bite all of me

So that I never wake up again, not at least in this life

And even if I wake up, all I want is this pain to terminate

I end my day with a sigh, somewhat that of relief

I tell myself not every day is supposed to be good

Some days I might as well have to question my beliefs.

Cussing, cursing, swearing, none of that could soothe me,

Hence all I did that day was let the bedbugs bite all of me.

The next day I wake up and find myself in the same state,

I do my chores and make myself get out of bed, unmotivated.

I tell myself the same old lies, which no longer made any sense

Which no longer were supposed to give me an energy boost.

I wish I had a friend by my side, to tackle with all this weariness

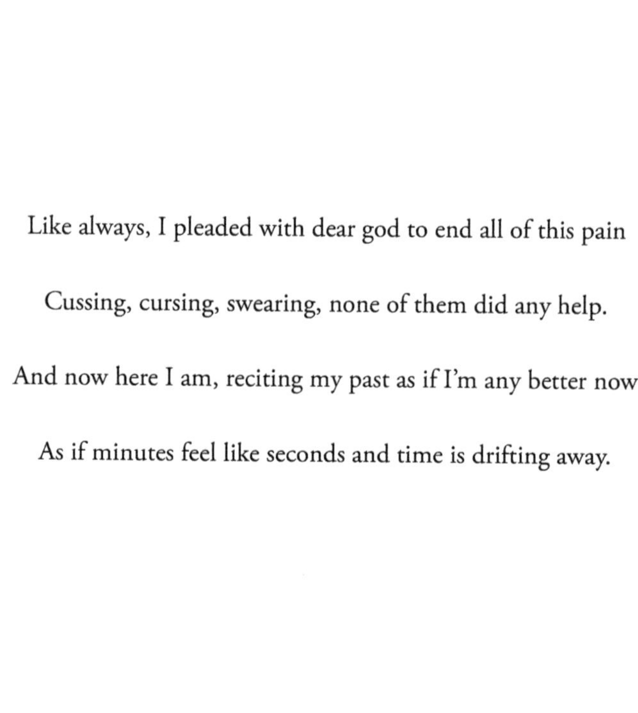

Like always, I pleaded with dear god to end all of this pain

Cussing, cursing, swearing, none of them did any help.

And now here I am, reciting my past as if I'm any better now

As if minutes feel like seconds and time is drifting away.

When worlds collide

You spend the first few years of your life, in solitude,

Wondering when you'd find a person who'd be "yours"

Someone who would devote the rest of his life to you

A living entity, made of flesh and blood, willing to stick with you until the very end.

You wait and wait and wait— as if your wait is perpetual, incessant.

And right when you begin to give up on your hopes

There he comes, crashing in; composing a song and humming it in your ears all day.

Making the first move, as though he waited all his life to witness his world collide with yours.

You are left speechless, substantiating his intrinsic ability to hold you spellbound.

And you never end a day without wondering what you did to deserve him.

I found a letter that went like…

"You say…

You say you love me, then why do you hurt me?

I'm just too helpless despite knowing you love me.

It doesn't seem right to let you drift away from me

But you actions leave me shattered and irreparable

And now I wonder what one does after being broken.

You say it's alright but how's holding grudges alright?

There were reasons to leave you when I did

Ironically, I see none for you to do the same now

So I ask myself why you're so keen on avenging me

Perhaps it's just a human's tendency to break his vow.

You say I lift your mood each day but I know I don't

Hence now I'll follow the path of "silent treatment"

And get going, to get a life and be a part of this world.

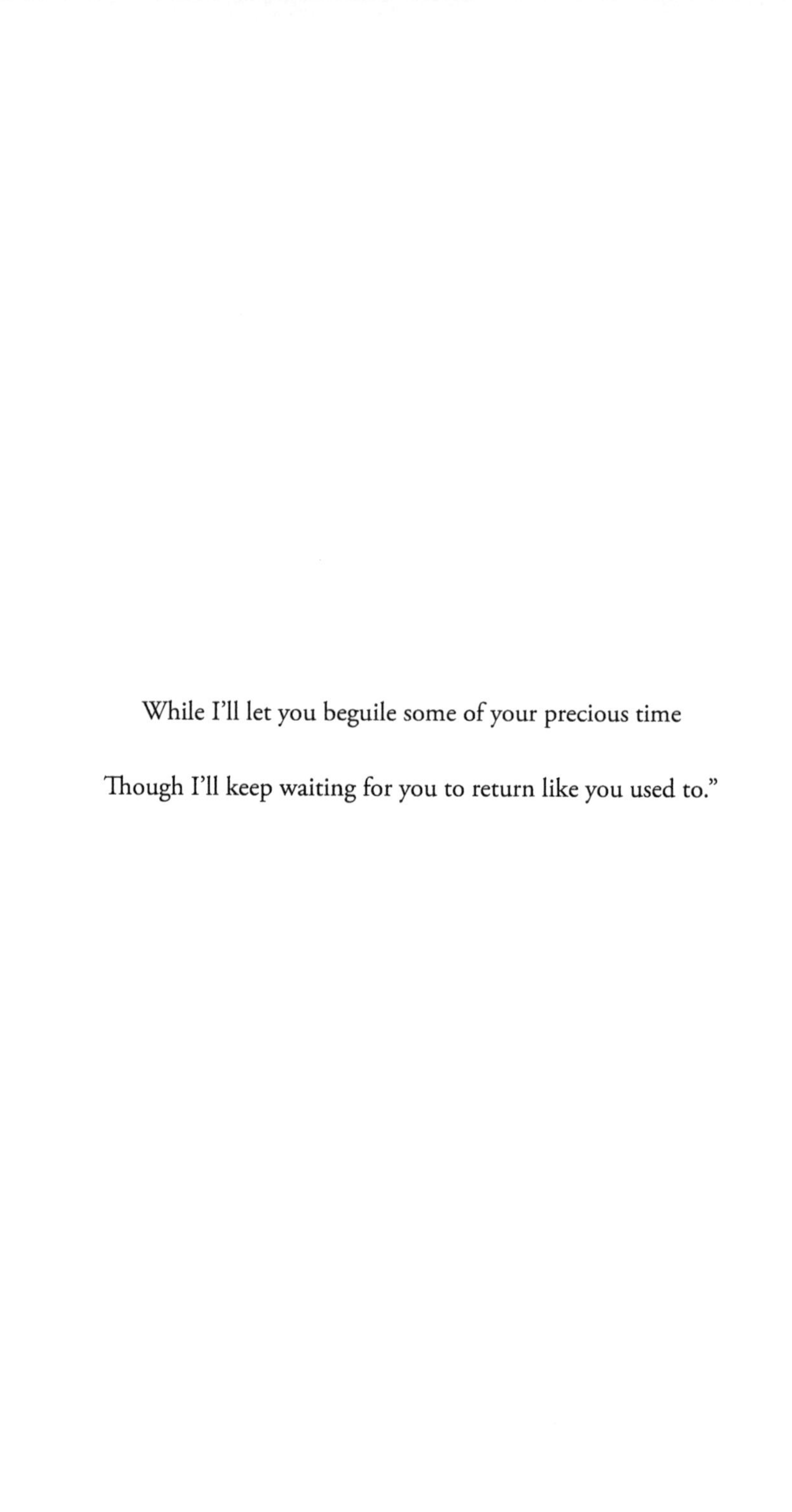

While I'll let you beguile some of your precious time

Though I'll keep waiting for you to return like you used to."

A girl I met made a wish that didn't go unheard:

"I made a wish upon the moons of Jupiter

One that could not be fulfilled by that of Earth

One that needed sheer luck and fortune

For making me & you "us" again.

I hoped we could be together this one time

I wanted to see that smile on our faces

The one that faded long ago when we parted

The one that needs to be seen again.

I knew something needed a fix

And that remedy wasn't available as a wish

Upon our goddamned moon

Though I tried just to fall flat on my face.

I wished for a new, golden opportunity

For changing our fates at this very moment

& yet I know life's not a fairytale bliss,

& that no one can be this disingenuous.

Call it a foolish or false hope,

Call it me being overcredulous & sanguine.

But that's what I feel about the two of us

That there's a fix for us to be one soon."

-would my wish not go unheard too if I wish upon the moons of Jupiter?

Did we lock eyes from two worlds apart or…

Did we lock them across the subway tracks?

I. The last time we met,

You said it's over.

Did you think enough

To come to such a closure?

Guess you were too immature

To grasp my feelings for you.

Just so you know, that very same day,

I spent the rest of my time

Wondering where

The curve was drawn on our line.

You kept ignoring me,
Averting your gaze from me,

As if trying hard enough to

Divert yourself towards

The unrealistic haze.

I went bonkers later

Sobbed my heart out

Made a pact

To never fall for mere words

Again…

II. Then one fine day

Months later,

Whilst I was crossing

The street,

I felt your presence again.

I sensed your phoniness,

I sighted your anatomy.

Trying to run away

From the person

Who made me lose my sanity,

I was well determined,

To not fall for you again.

But amidst the hustle-bustle

Of the city

There were the two of us.

You expecting a patch up

Me sticking to my soliloquy.

However, in the end,

It was you who won the game,

As we locked eyes again…

Plot twist: it wasn't a "he" anymore…

I got introduced to new terms

Love knows no boundaries

And neither does the month of **June**

Hence people chose it as

A month to celebrate the boon!

Midst of streets we descry pride,

As **“they”** find love in the sky.

They have the rainbow by their side,

In the flags which can be seen soaring high!

There’s so much to show **pride** for,

That they can’t quite admire every day.

Hence June’s the month they chose,

To showcase the pride of being **gay**!

The summer month passes soon,

With them spreading the word of love.

Isn't it a sublime blessing from heaven,

That they keep fulfilling the behove?

Fast forward to October

October 1st-

The long-lost charm is now being brought back,

People have once again been reunited.

Laugher, joy & ecstasy, all of which were lacked,

Now, in the fair, could easily be sighted.

The city of happiness might not be ours,

But what is ours can very well be nurtured.

The way people were offering each other flowers,

As if the town was never looted by a lurcher.

If only this moment could be extended,

Until tomorrow the world would be a better place.

Yet we know it's just a festival, soon to be ended,

The "now" people have, has to be embraced.

October 2nd-

Days like this,

When I'm taken over by regrets,

So many of them

Reverberating inside my head.

A voice from within

Asking me to imagine the life;

One that I'd have been leading

If I'd lifted the knife.

I wish to banish from today

But I'm sadly just a fragile human

Made of flesh and blood.

Nonetheless, I'm breathing

Alive, and grateful

For the times I've had a shoulder

When life seemed too hateful.

However, my thought process

Never ceases to tell me

Just how despicable today is;

And how better off dead I'd be.

- The happiest moments arrive unexpectedly but so do the saddest ones.

Lava of hate (speaking from experience)

Not that anyone cares but have a taste of what others saw me as (answer: a competitor)

There was a time when we used to be good, close friends. I reckoned you as one of my confidants. Soon you'd earned the appellation of "magnanimity". Perhaps that was a huge title and I should've waited longer to taste the venom in your heart, the bona fide jealousy burning inside layered with sugary lips and mushy conduct on top of it. Your true feelings could never be expressed, revealed, or exposed with false words intended for flattery and cajolery. And so I got fooled, unaware of your intramural intentions.

I thought being with someone for a long time makes you attached to them and you begin to want to change yourself for them. Perhaps I was wrong now that within a month's time, the almighty had acquainted me with the reality and the fact that I could never ever disguise myself as a comrade holding a sword in my back. The way you backstabbed me holding authentic power within your hands was worth watching. I might have to spend the rest of my life trying to heal, digesting whatever happened was all my fault and getting over someone who called me their friend just for the sake of it.

It's been years now and it's a shame that I still haven't been able to move on. I still haven't been able to replace you with a person who deserves someone as true as me. The hole you carved within my heart could perhaps never be filled and I'll have to live the rest of my life knowing that I won't have somebody to fill that void in me. Honestly speaking, I don't even want to use someone for such a purpose. For in the end, unlike yours, the blood that courses through my veins doesn't make me want to give birth to a lava of hate.

Still alive… And hopeful

In the darkest of days

We strive to find some rays

Rays of hope, they say

To keep our horrors at bay.

Got used to unpredictability by now...

The sweet cool breeze and bitter harsh winds

Plotting a future for the leaves stuck in the linds

Creatures, big and small enjoy their breaths

As I sense uncertainty among the shallowest depths

After the rain, it all has however been kept at bay

Until another such unpredictable grey day.

Another form of art

I've tried

Falling

From the highest tops,

Hoping it would be the

End of me.

Yet here I am,

Telling the story

Of how

I

Survived Without thee.

I've dipped my pen In red ink,

To write a note

Having an abrupt ending,

But it was all a Waste of time,

For all I required

Was some mending.

A part of me

Was dead way back,

But the pieces that remained

Brought me back to my senses

And it felt as though a N E W life was gained.

Nobody caught me when I fell

but me

Hence without a doubt, I hereby say

I am , I was and I will be

My own knight

And continue this fight

Just another lonely day I guess

It wasn't until Saturday morning

That I realized I'd been sleeping this entire week.

The first thing I checked was my phone.

Zero notifications. Zero calls.

The only question I asked myself was

"What difference does me being alive make

To everyone's lifestyle?"

With the least bit of energy, I got out of bed.

Did my chores

And traipsed towards my garden.

"This stinks", I thought.

I thanked my stinky green foliage

For acknowledging my absence.

Let me live my lies in peace

Whilst I am alive

Let me live my fantasies

For life ain't one to spare

It goes and goes

And fades away

Amidst all this perplexity

I stand astride

Loitering for a miracle

Though it may not transpire

It's not even like I care

Midst of uncertainty

I feed myself these lies

On behalf of you

As circadian necessities

Lies, they are, mind it

Didst I not adore you

Once upon a time

All I now have

For you, is loathing

Can't bear this anymore.

A turning point in my new life

I once went to a fortune teller

To know if the future favors me

And enquire about my lines of fate

To learn of what awaits me.

Upon entering her place,

I was already feeling better

Than before when I kept sulking

Prior to when I received my letter.

But oh, I saw a queue of people

Waiting to have their futures revealed

So I thought it well to join them

And be a part of the ones to appeal.

I waited and waited and waited

Until when at last it was my turn

To have the life ahead of me judged

And know what's it left to be earned.

The woman stood up to welcome me

Into the house of fools, she said

I was baffled as to why she said so

Thought if I had been misled.

And finally when she started speaking,

Instead of doing the usual palm reading,

She made me aware of the present

And the opportunities I could be heeding.

She said, "The future isn't to be played with.

The present is what you can ponder

And last but not the least

Destiny is yours to create and conquer"

Her words seemed to leave an impact

On me. For success seemed too near.

The present which I steered clear of

Paved the way to a beautiful future.

Wrote to her in a long time

"Your eyes, embodiments of the ocean,
Which I may anytime drown in.
Your ears, curved like a labyrinth,
That make me want to get lost.
Your nose, clearly craving another,
For a kiss, like that of the Eskimos.
Your skin, awaiting a warm touch,
That you, too, have been deprived of.
Your voice, as comforting as the patter,
That I can lie listening to, for eternities.
Your lips, just like honey, so nectarous.
Which I choke back my drool for.
And you yourself are everything, my love.
For you keep taking my breath away."

I pitied myself…

…because my heart is now a haunted house,
Where spirits of my past lovers keep wandering,
In search of a fragile spot to aim and kill,
And make peace with their evil minds.
This heart of mine does not know to be kind,
Or to be merciful as it used to be once upon a time,
When it thought of love to be a bliss
To be a process that results in permanence.
It has been taught and trained for way too long
As initially intended by those evil brains.
To be cold and not recall the human traits
Other than misery, trickery and treachery.
But no matter how spooky it seems from the outside,
Someone, someday may just notice the fragility that lies
And cover up for all the previous betrayals
So that the frightened heart decides to come out
And make up for all those years of callousness.
But until then, it shall keep itself locked in the chest
And not reject the rumours that had been spread
Of it being just another haunted house
Where the people should not dare to step in.

No escape

Who could have ever thought
A fragile human like me could resort to mettle
To let my sanity be plucked and shattered
And witnessing the unforgettable was-
Beyond my and your consternation.
Looking back now in time, it's crystal clear
How the overestimation has let "us" go kaput.
And without any bias, there is no one but me to blame.
For as dicey as the situation may have seemed,
The decision was arbitrarily mine
And life has now been cornered to the bare minimum
With me having pushed myself towards the dark void
From where there seems no escape.

I decided to take a walk

I went for a stroll, by the lake.
In the cold winter morning,
When others were reluctant
To even get out of their beds.

I saw a ray of hope,
With the first morning light;
That gestured me to stay strong,
And look forward to a better day.

I found the same old lake,
To be tranquil, and glossy-
As if waiting for the stones,
To hit the surface and form ripples.

I then shifted my gaze,
Towards the lush green trees.
And found a nest with two eggs,
With the unborn, eager to finally see.

I was all ears for the nature, too,
So I listened to the chirps-
Of the birds that were nearby,

Off to hunt for some food.

As I continued to admire nature,
The roads might've gotten envious.
For it was them I was walking upon;
Whose existence was undeniable.

Soon, others were stepping in,
After having missed the sights,
That kept capturing my attention
Until I reached back to my home.

I also got hands on someone else's phone and read a text that said

"Boy, believe me or not, I've waited long enough

To experience the love that you're giving away.

Seems like I've been patient for eternities now

And that virtue is making my dreams come to play.

Ah! You're finally painting my monochrome life

With colours I'd once listed under my favourites.

And the life which I once wanted to put a pause to

Is the same I now want to share as a whole with you."

PS- no, I didn't steal the phone or anything...

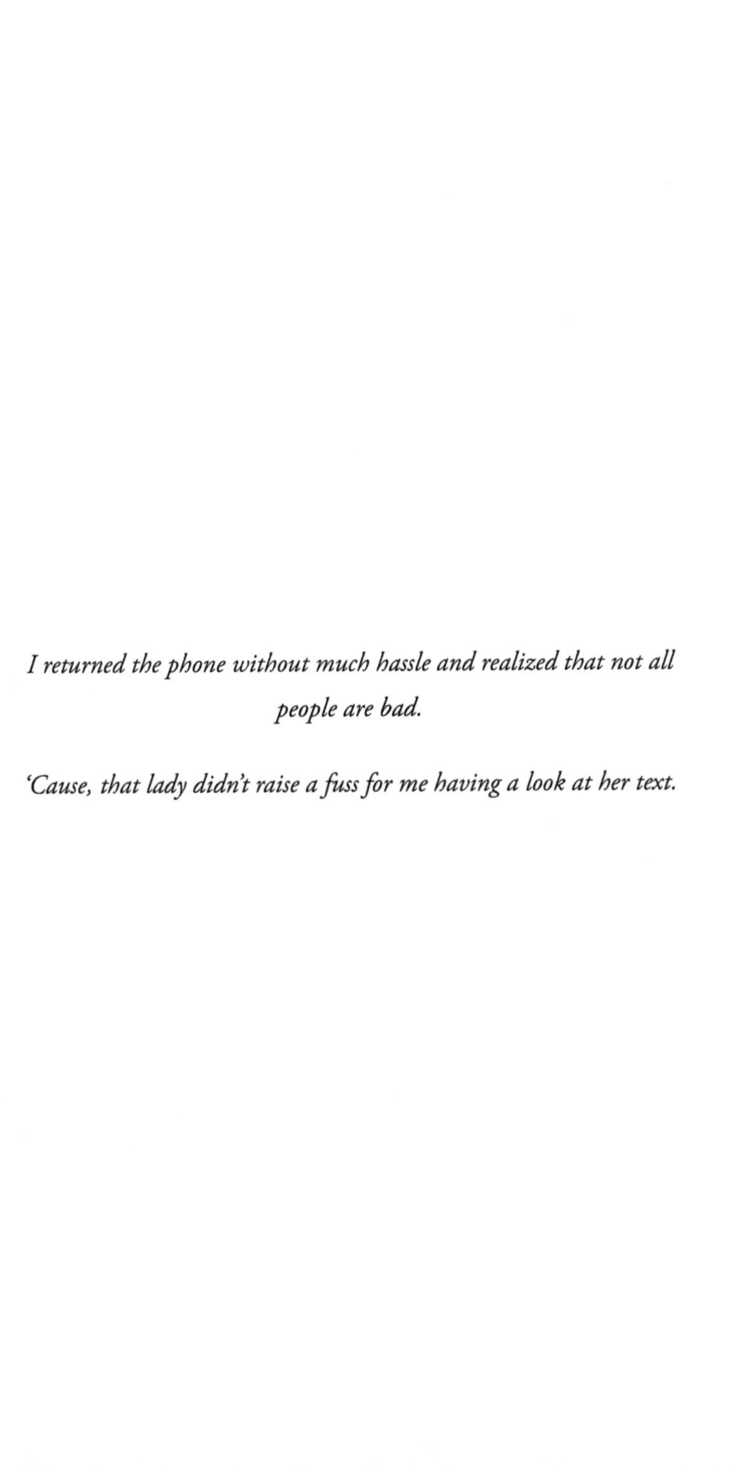

I returned the phone without much hassle and realized that not all people are bad.

'Cause, that lady didn't raise a fuss for me having a look at her text.

So I wrote a letter to my arch enemy

"Let me for once be in your place,

Let me know what it feels like to be on top.

Appealing?

Just so you know, I've been working hard for years now.

And so it's somewhat becoming mundane to know that I can't even match your pace.

For I know not what to do with myself if I can't even break that vow.

It's been years and I know not how it feels to be on top.

The last time I saw myself over there was among some doofuses.

Now being surrounded by a crowd of geniuses makes me feel worthless.

Is it that I really can't reach your position,

Or will it just be a fluke even if I do?

I've been working on myself for ages now, probably ages more to come.

And success hasn't knocked on my door yet,

Although there are some people craving to stand where I do.

It might just be appealing from far, but it does feel scandalous to know

That you're not on top but just whirling around the top.

How dear you hold your level that I've been buzzing nearby

For a long long time. It's been years now and I can't keep going like this,

If I can't taste your position by myself, for once, be my savior, let me be over there.

I do know it's too much to ask of a favor. But you've been there, standing on top

For years now, and if you can't let me be there, I stay surrounded

By a limited few possibilities. And I don't want to get into the details.

For you may not see me, ever again."

I learnt to laugh!

“There resides a spirit in that dark room”, said my mother as I watched her feed my little brother a mouthful of hoaxes.

Earlier that day I was being given a lesson on why kids should not be misguided.

“Is it him who’s being misguided or is it me who knows and prefers to remain close-mouthed?”, I asked myself.

The day passed like any other day and losing track of time, I realized it was 11:00 PM.

“11 more minutes”, I mimped.

It was soon 11:11 and I made a wish.

“May I have the audacity to speak up and reveal what lies underneath. That what my brother learned today about spirits is false. This is just called following the path of unorthodoxy.”

It was 11:11 and I, a thirteen-year-old, made a wish.

Who’s the nincompoop here that needs proper guidance? A five-year-old being taught about supernatural things to remain entertained or a grown-up thirteen-year-old believing in the magical moment of 11:11? I laughed for the first time in this life,

that too while thinking of how stupid I was.

To you, the living

My last few words

As I rest my head

Might just juxtapose my entire life of misery.

It doesn't feel right to leave,

but rather live.

Now that I look back,

life was beautiful,

far more beautiful than what I knew

But it turns out that we only appreciate things after they're gone.

I'm glad I survived those rough days and I hope you all will, too.

A piece of advice:

Cherish what you have now

For there might be some hidden melodies that do not sparkle.

And that one last day is all it takes for you to realize

The love The lost The connection

The love:

Those selected people reveal it's all serendipitous

But most die keeping within

Appreciate that "love"

For that perfect moment, you've been waiting for

Might just fade away in an instant.

The lost:

Raise a toast to that one love of yours

Who didn't wait for your confession

And hence led a life devoid of (a.k.a sans) love

The connection:

Might just be a kinship

Or that worn away relationship, for you never know

If that's the last connection you ever feel.

My last few words,

To the living

That I can't ever physically come in contact with.

Take your time to go for walks

By the lake

Alongside that rectangular park.

And appreciate what you have,

Even what you don't

For you never know who you may lose today,

Or who may lose you someday?

By December I had learnt what "delicacies" were

Sweater weather. Steamed baths. Mocha cravings.
Foggy breaths. Dewy leaves.
Blanket snuggles. Dry skins. Awaited sunbeams.
All of which, are delicacies
Cracking up
When winter decides to finally give a knock.
To finally let the lonesome find company
In their sweaters, in their baths, in their cups,
In their quilts, skins, etc, etc.
To let them find warmth, and love.
And peace. And solitude.
But deep down, they know,
How this comfort isn't everlasting. Nothing is perennial.
It's just a matter of days,
Until they have to let go of the warmth.
Until they have to lose it to the other hemisphere.
And struggle to fit in with the upcoming season.

Special thanks,

To my beloved spirts
Who used to haunt me at night
And still do

www.ingramcontent.com/pod-product-compliance
Ingram Content Group UK Ltd.
Pitfield, Milton Keynes, MK11 3LW, UK
UKHW040010200726
13854UKWH00001B/135